Live a joyful life!
Blessed Be!

Lyon ☺

An Ordinary Girl

A

MAGICAL CHILD

by W. Lyon Martin

To my very own
darling "Rabbit," who
encouraged me every
step of the way.

Pagan World Press
a division of Dubsar House Publishing
www.dubsarhouse.com

An Ordinary Girl, A Magical Child

The illustrations were created in watercolor, gouache and pencil on 140lb Kilimanjaro cold press. Text was set in Palatino. Cover lettering was hand painted using Bandolero.

People who want to be part of the Circle gather around the space. We may sing a special song to help people concentrate. That is called "Grounding." We ground so our energy isn't spread out. This connects us to the Earth. It gives us more energy for Magic.

Next is "Closing the Circle." We imagine an invisible wall. It will hold energy in until it is sent where we want. The wall also keeps other energy out. We call the four directions. Each direction is a different element. North is Earth. East is Air. South is Fire. West is Water. Pagans do this because the Elements help protect us when we do our Magic.

We thank the Elements for watching when we are done. We say goodbye. We call this "Opening the Circle."

The Wheel of the Year

Pagans have special holy days that are different from everybody else. The Earth and the Seasons are important to Pagans. That is what Pagan holidays are for. We have holy days for the Sun, called Sabbats. We have eight Sabbats. The Pagan New Year is on October 31. Halloween falls on the same day as Samhain. Samhain is pronounced "sow-en."

Winter
Yule Dec. 20, 21 or 22
Brigid February 2
Samhain October 31-Nov 1
Ostara March 20, 21 or 22
Spring
Fall
Beltane May 1
Mabon Sept. 20, 21 or 22
Lammas August 1
Litha June 20, 21 or 22
Summer

February 2nd is Imbolc. This is the same day as Groundhog Day. Imbolc means "in the belly". This is when sheep are almost ready to have baby lambs. February 2nd is also called the Feast of Light. Pagans celebrate this day because winter is almost over. The days are longer.

Rabbit goes seed shopping with Mommy. This is her favorite thing. Mommy lets her pick any flowers she wants. They go home to plant the seeds in cups. Mommy, Daddy and Rabbit thank Goddess for bringing back the light. They ask Her to help the seedlings grow strong. Rabbit waters the seeds carefully everyday. Soon, they will grow enough to plant outside.

Rabbit Has A Bad Day

"Mommy!" Rabbit called.

Mommy walked into the child care center. Rabbit ran and leaped into Mommy's arms. She was very happy to see her. Mommy placed Rabbit back on her feet. She kissed the top of her head.

Mommy said, "Rabbit, remember your book bag and lunch box. Is your homework done?" Rabbit nodded.

Mommy took Rabbit's hand in her own. They headed out to the car to drive home. As soon as they got into the car, Rabbit started to sniffle.

"Mommy," she said, "today was a very bad day."

Then she burst into tears.

"What happened?" Mommy asked.

Rabbit sniffed a great big sniff. "It was awful, Mommy. The kids were so mean, the teacher tried to stop them but they wouldn't. They kept doing it, even when we went to music class. They teased me. All the kids were mean to me."

Mommy parked the car in the driveway and got out. She pulled Rabbit to her holding her close.

"Tell me what happened from the beginning," she said gently.

"Well," started Rabbit. "Teacher taught us about Groundhog Day today. But before she did, she asked if anyone knew what today was. I held up my hand. She picked me. I was so excited, because we were going to plant our seeds today, I said Imbolc. Everybody laughed at me. No one had ever heard of Imbolc, not even Teacher. She asked me to explain what I was talking about. I couldn't, 'cause all the kids were laughing. I wanted to cry. Teacher tried to make everybody stop. She told them I wasn't Christian. I celebrate different holidays. That's when Tim and John started saying I didn't believe in God. They said I was going to go to a bad place when I died." Rabbit sniffled.

Mommy hugged Rabbit.

"You do believe in God, don't you, Honey?" she asked.

Rabbit nodded.

"And you believe in Goddess, too, right?" Mommy said.

Rabbit nodded again.

"You also believe Goddess and God love you. They want you to be happy and healthy. They won't send you to a bad place even if you forget about Them."

Rabbit looked shocked. "I'd never forget about Them, Mommy," she said firmly. "They would never do anything mean to me like send me to a bad place."

She snuggled deeper into Mommy's arms.

"Next time those boys start teasing you, just tell them you do too believe in God. Say God believes in you and will keep you safe forever," Mommy said into the top of Rabbit's head.

Rabbit felt better. Mommy was so good at making her feel better. She wouldn't let anybody tease her about not being Christian; she didn't have to be Christian to believe in God. God didn't pick people because of their religions, He picked them because they were kind and did what their Mommy and Daddy asked them to. Rabbit smiled.

"And Goddess too," she thought to herself.

The next day on the playground, when Tim and John started to tease her again, Rabbit told them what Mommy said. They stopped teasing her. Tim shrugged his shoulders, then as a ball rolled by him, he grabbed it and ran off. John glanced at Rabbit and followed behind his friend.

They didn't tease Rabbit about God any more.

Spring Equinox ~ Ostara

March 21st is the Spring Equinox. Sometimes the Equinox can be on the 20th. Other times it falls on the 22nd. Day and night are the same lengths. Daddy plants the garden with early crops like lettuce and carrots. Rabbit lives up to her name when the first leaves poke out from the dark earth. She nibbles on baby spinach leaves and tiny peas, which are sweet as sugar. She'd eat them all if Mommy didn't watch her!

Mommy and Rabbit celebrate the Equinox. They get up very early to watch the sun rise. They wait. They see the round ball of yellow rise. They take handfuls of oats and sprinkle them into the air.

Mommy says, "We give food to Mother Earth. God and Goddess will make sure we have enough food, too. It is important to take care of the Earth. Without a healthy Earth, there will be no food or water."

Rabbit remembers Mommy and Daddy give food to soup kitchens. "Is feeding other people part of feeding God and Goddess?"

Mommy smiled, "Yes, because we are all part of Goddess and God. They are part of all of us."

Beltane

Rabbit pulled on new pink stockings. Mommy had taken her shopping for a dress. Rabbit smoothed the ruffled skirt. She looked closely at the flowers on her puffy sleeves. She liked the noise the dress made when she moved. It made her feel grown up. She couldn't wait to show it off at the Beltane celebration. Mommy and Daddy were taking her. It was the first day in May. The day had begun cloudy. Rabbit worried Mommy and Daddy would decide to stay home. The sun finally came out. It was warm enough so they wouldn't need sweaters.

Rabbit grinned. This was the best Spring holiday. Mommy and Daddy stayed home most holidays. This celebration needed lots of people to be fun. Her family would go to a big park. Many other Pagan families would be there after lunch. Everyone would dance and sing. There would be stories, too.

Rabbit thought about how the men always dug a deep hole for a very tall staff. Someone always brought one to be the Maypole. Rabbit darted into the hallway. She checked the basket of ribbons. Mommy bought the yards of multi-colored ribbon at the store. Everyone would pick out a ribbon. They would tie each ribbon onto the top of the Maypole. The men would hoist the pole up. They would put the other end into the deep hole. There was always a lot of joking about getting the pole straight up. They would make sure the dirt was packed tight around the bottom. The pole had to stay up during the dance. All the dancers would grab their ribbons. Some people would dance clockwise. Rabbit's family says Sun-Wise. The others would dance counter clockwise.

Rabbit was thrilled. Mommy decided Rabbit wouldn't be stepped on this year. Rabbit would join the Maypole dance in her new dress.

Rabbit held nervously onto her ribbon. She listened to High Priest and Priestess asking the fairies and their Queen to come dance with all the people. Rabbit knew she wouldn't really see any Faery Folk. But she thought she could feel them coming on the flower-scented breeze.

The dance started slowly. In and out, up and down went the ribbons. Their bright colors wove together at the top of the Maypole. The people went faster around the Maypole. The colored ribbons wove together around the pole. They moved closer to the bottom. Their shortening length pulled the dancers closer to each other. They made a tighter circle around the pole. Still faster they danced. There were shouts of laughter.

Other people who were not dancing, started clapping. They shouted encouragement to the dancers, who were getting tired. The dance was almost done. People began to trip as they danced around the pole. They gasped for breath between giggles. Some people ran out of ribbon. They left the circle. The others danced until they finish wrapping the rest of their ribbons around the Maypole.

Rabbit lost hold of her ribbon. It had gotten too short for her to hold. She backed up carefully away from the remaining dancers. She fell into a pile on the grass. She was laughing very hard. Mommy came to hug her tight. Daddy ruffled her hair. He handed her a cup of water. Rabbit gulped the water thirstily.

Summer Solstice ~ Litha

The days get longer until the end of June. This is the Summer Solstice. The holiday falls on June 20th, 21st or 22nd. The sun is strongest on the Solstice. The night is the shortest of the year. This is the first day of summer. This is also the start of the coming winter. The days grow shorter after the Solstice. This holiday is about letting go. Pagans let go of things they no longer need. Letting go isn't the same as throwing things away. We let go of something in our life because we have outgrown it. That means we have something new coming into our lives. Our planting now changes into harvesting.

A House Blessing

Summer is coming. Mommy invited friends from the city to come help with the yearly home blessing. They come every year. Before they arrive Mommy, Daddy and Rabbit clean every room of the house. The floors are washed and waxed. Even the cats' litter boxes are scrubbed. When the whole house from top to bottom is shiny and clean, the house is ready for the ritual.

Mommy, Daddy, SeyWitch and Thoss sat in the living room sipping iced tea while they discussed the blessing ritual. SeyWitch pulled an ancient bell out of her big bag. She handed it to Rabbit. Rabbit shook it gently. It rang clear and loud even though Rabbit had barely moved it.

SeyWitch smiled. "Would you like to use my bell during the ritual?"

Rabbit's eyes got all round. She glanced at Mommy.

"Oh, really? Can I really use your bell, SeyWitch?"

Mommy nodded, smiling.

"Thank you, thank you!!!!"

Rabbit bounced up from the floor and jumped into SeyWitch's lap. SeyWitch was her favorite of Mommy's Pagan friends. She knew all about things like Fairies and what the birds said when they talked to each other.

They all got up to start the house blessing. Mommy briefly told the others what to say. Rabbit held onto Seywitch's bell. She would ring it during the ritual in the house while the adults chanted. They started at the front door. Thoss made a pentagram in the air in front of the door. Daddy sprinkled the door with the salt water he'd blessed before the ritual.

Mommy started to chant.

"Greetings to those who guard my walls. Many thanks for your protection and care. I give you friendship and praise."

Everyone chanted with her. Rabbit rang the bell to help chase away negative energy.

Mommy led the way through the house. Following the outer wall Sun-Wise, they moved through the living room toward the kitchen. At each window or door, Thoss drew a pentacle in the air. Daddy sprinkled more salt water. Into the dining room, to the bathroom, the bedrooms and down into the basement and back up again to the spot where they started. Rabbit rang the bell the entire time while everyone continued to chant. She chanted, too.

Mommy pulled open the front door and they all followed her out into the yard. Daddy put down the salt water and picked up a bowl of corn flour that was on the porch. Mommy changed the words in the chant slightly.

"Greetings to those who guard these boundaries. Many thanks for your protection and care. I give you friendship and praise."

She began to walk down the sidewalk to the front of the property, turned to her right and walked across the grass in front of the house. She chanted all the while. Daddy came behind her, sprinkling a trail of corn flour at the edge of the grass. Everyone chanted with Mommy as they walked down one side of the yard and across to the other.

As they approached the mailbox, Seywitch said, "Put some of the corn flour inside so you always get good news."

Rabbit thought that was something only SeyWitch could know. After all, she is a mailwoman.

They were back on the porch now. They all held hands in a small circle. Mommy smiled at Rabbit. Rabbit knew she had done well with her part of the ritual. She smiled back.

"Once again our boundaries are strong. Our guardians are fed and remembered. With the blessings of Goddess and God, may the coming year bring health and prosperity to this home. So mote it be," said Mommy.

"So mote it be," said everyone else.

Mommy opened the front door. Rabbit smelled the aroma of good food as they went inside to eat.

Lughnasadh

The first of the three harvest festivals is called Lughnasadh (loo-na-sa). Lughnasadh happens on August 1. Pagans celebrate the first fruits on this Sabbat. Rabbit's family has a ritual with apples dipped in honey. Rabbit, Mommy and Daddy take turns covering juicy apple slices with golden honey. Rabbit, Mommy and Daddy say a thank you with each crunchy bite. They are always very sticky when they are done with the apples. They are happy to have so much in their lives to be thankful for.

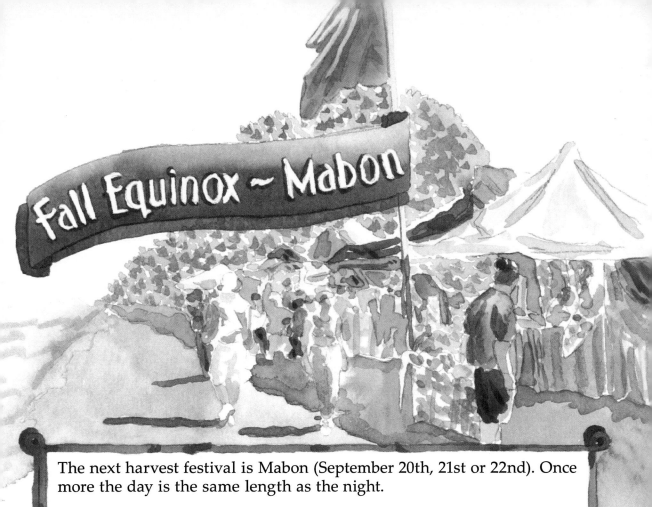

Fall Equinox ~ Mabon

The next harvest festival is Mabon (September 20th, 21st or 22nd). Once more the day is the same length as the night.

Before most people got their food from the supermarket, they had to plant their own food. This time of year was when many of the crops they planted were ready for harvest. Grandma starts to can all the vegetables Daddy and Grandpa planted in the spring. The tomatoes are ripening faster than Daddy can pick them and it seems like there is much more than any one could possibly eat. Rabbit knows even though it looks like a lot, all the cans will be empty when she and Mommy plant the seeds again next year for Imbolc.

This is a holiday when the Pagans where Rabbit lives have a huge picnic. All different kinds of Pagans gather together. They have a fair. There are people selling things in booths, like clothes, herbs, ritual tools or incense. Artists and musicians show off their arts. There are storytelling and crafts for the children. The adults have drumming circles. The celebration lasts for two days. There is a public circle at the beginning and another one at the end of the weekend.

Samhain ~ Halloween

Rabbit spun around in front of the mirror, watching the skirt of her costume twirl around her ankles. She checked to make sure her wings were still straight. They looked good to her. She patted the shoulder straps then ran from the room.

Mommy waited downstairs with a bag and flashlight. Rabbit giggled. Today was Halloween.

All over town children were putting on costumes for trick or treating. Rabbit knew they didn't know they were celebrating a Pagan holiday, but she liked to pretend they did. Once a year, she thought it was nice that the other children celebrated the same holiday she did. Being different was hard.

Halloween for Rabbit's family is trick or treating with costumes, but it is also something special.

It is the Pagan New Year. It is a time of endings. It is a time of beginnings.

This is the holiday when Rabbit's family remembers their friends and family who have died and crossed over into Summer Land. That is the place many Pagans believe we go after we die.

Mommy, Daddy and Rabbit sorted through the piles of candy collected from the houses in the neighborhood. They made two piles. One they put in the big green bowl. Rabbit knew there'd be enough to last almost until Yule. She grinned. The other pile would go on the altar for Goddess and God. Mommy and Daddy would add their own offerings after Rabbit was sleeping.

Rabbit proudly carried the offering bowl to the altar. Mommy lit candles. She told a story about the summers she spent at her Grandma's house when she was a little girl. Mommy cried a little bit as she shared her memory. Rabbit barely remembered her great grandmother. But she did remember how sad Mommy had been when Granny died. She watched solemnly until Mommy finished. Mommy laughed then. She tousled Rabbit's hair.

"Why the long face, Rabbit?" she asked. "Granny is coming to visit me. The veil between the Worlds of the Living and Dead will be thin tonight. If I am very quiet and still, she can tell me how much she loves me."

Rabbit grinned, "I know, Mommy."

They watched the candles on the altar for a while. Then they all went into the kitchen to eat pumpkin muffins still warm from the oven.

Winter Solstice ~ Yule

The last of the eight holidays is Yule. Winter Solstice is the longest night of the year. Many Pagan families light lots of candles. They stay up until the Sun rises in the morning. Not Rabbit's family, Mommy and Daddy have to work. Rabbit has to go to school. Sometimes Mommy will let Rabbit stay up late if Solstice falls on a weekend. Mommy will keep candles burning all night. Those are special Solstices. There is always a small pile of presents under the Yule tree. This year Mommy asked Rabbit to say a prayer asking Goddess and God to bring back the Sun. Rabbit scrunched up her face. She thought hard. Rabbit didn't want to say prayers. She wanted to open presents. Mommy said she could open a present for every sentence. Rabbit thought that sounded fair.

"Goddess," she said, "Bless me with the light of the Sun." She looked at Mommy and Daddy. Mommy smiled. Rabbit opened a present.

"God," Rabbit recited, "Thank you for a warm house to live in." Daddy handed her another wrapped box.

Rabbit grinned. This isn't so hard, she thought to herself. Six more times she thought of something to bring back the Sun. Soon she was knee deep in discarded wrapping paper and bows.

Mommy went to the bookshelf to get the big book of Pagan stories. Rabbit shoved her presents under the tree. She'd play with them later. Now Mommy was going to read the story of the rebirth of the Sun. It was her favorite Pagan story. Rabbit jumped onto the couch to snuggle close to Mommy and Daddy.

Pagans celebrate the different phases of the Moon. We call these holy days Esbats. These ceremonies are celebrated at night. It is easier to see the Moon at night. There are 8 phases of the Moon. Each one has its own name. Rabbit's family keeps track of the quarter Moon phases. They are the Full, Waxing, Waning and the Dark (or New) Moon. A Waxing Moon means the portion of the Moon we see in the sky is getting larger. It is halfway between the Dark and Full Moons. A Waning Moon is one that is getting smaller, halfway between the Full and Dark Moons.

The phases of the Moon also are linked to the 3 faces of Goddess. The first tiny sliver until just before the Full Moon is the time of the Maiden. She holds the power of beginnings and learning new things. The Full Moon is the time of the Mother. This is the time for working on projects already started or bringing abundance into your life. Next is the Old One. She is the Crone. Now is the time of the waning and Dark Moon. It is a time of secrets and healings.

Pagans believe each phase of the Moon has special energies. Many Pagans will only do certain types of Magic during a particular phase of the Moon. They believe Full Moon energy is different than Dark Moon energy. Some Pagans, like Rabbit's family, will do a ritual or make Magic anytime during the month. Mommy just writes a ritual for the energy of that kind of Moon. The Moon energy follows the Moon's phase. Before the Full Moon is growing energy. Then is the time to ask for things to come into our lives, like getting better grades in school. A Dark Moon is just the opposite. Then is the proper time to ask for things to leave our lives, like a bad habit we want to change.

Rabbit's family usually celebrates the Full Moon. They are so busy they only have time for one ritual a month. Occasionally they will add another ritual. Sometimes they will pray for healing for a sick friend or extra money to pay for an unexpected expense.

The Cycles of the Moon

Full Moon

Rabbit's family keeps a special bowl in the kitchen. Every day they add left over bread to the bowl. All month long the contents of the bowl grow until the night of the Full Moon. That was tonight.

Rabbit jumped up and down in the kitchen. If she jumped high enough, she could see how full the offering bowl was. Rabbit peeked once more at the pile of dried bread. Then she went to school.

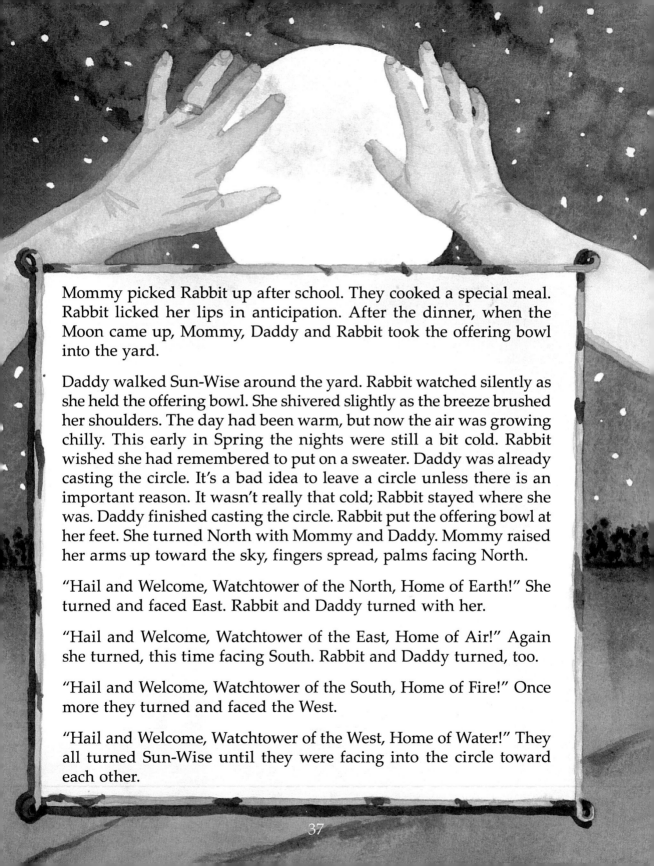

Mommy picked Rabbit up after school. They cooked a special meal. Rabbit licked her lips in anticipation. After the dinner, when the Moon came up, Mommy, Daddy and Rabbit took the offering bowl into the yard.

Daddy walked Sun-Wise around the yard. Rabbit watched silently as she held the offering bowl. She shivered slightly as the breeze brushed her shoulders. The day had been warm, but now the air was growing chilly. This early in Spring the nights were still a bit cold. Rabbit wished she had remembered to put on a sweater. Daddy was already casting the circle. It's a bad idea to leave a circle unless there is an important reason. It wasn't really that cold; Rabbit stayed where she was. Daddy finished casting the circle. Rabbit put the offering bowl at her feet. She turned North with Mommy and Daddy. Mommy raised her arms up toward the sky, fingers spread, palms facing North.

"Hail and Welcome, Watchtower of the North, Home of Earth!" She turned and faced East. Rabbit and Daddy turned with her.

"Hail and Welcome, Watchtower of the East, Home of Air!" Again she turned, this time facing South. Rabbit and Daddy turned, too.

"Hail and Welcome, Watchtower of the South, Home of Fire!" Once more they turned and faced the West.

"Hail and Welcome, Watchtower of the West, Home of Water!" They all turned Sun-Wise until they were facing into the circle toward each other.

Rabbit bent to lift the offering bowl. Now it was her turn. Tonight she was going to make the offering to Goddess and God. She had practiced her prayer all month. Mommy said she was old enough to do it on her own. Rabbit was nervous. What if she forgot something, or goofed up and said it all wrong? Then she remembered what Mommy and Daddy always told her. Goddess and God knew what was in her heart. The words were just to help her focus her thoughts. She relaxed a tiny bit. She still wanted to do it just right. It was the first time she was doing it all on her own. She wanted her parents to be proud of her.

Rabbit lifted the offering bowl high above her head.

She began her prayer. "Lord and Lady please accept my offering. Bring me peaceful dreams. Please help me not get mad or cry when the kids tease me at school." Rabbit asked, "This year, don't let the rabbits eat all the peas and lettuce Daddy and Grandpa just planted in the yard."

Repeating the phrase Mommy usually said, "May Your will be done for the best for all," she took the bread from the offering bowl and tossed it around the circle.